THE FALLACY OF NEUTRALITY.

AN ADDRESS

BY THE

HON. JOSEPH HOLT,

TO THE PEOPLE OF KENTUCKY,

DELIVERED AT LOUISVILLE, JULY 13TH, 1861;

ALSO

HIS LETTER TO J. F. SPEED, ESQ.

NEW YORK:
JAMES G. GREGORY,
(SUCCESSOR TO W. A. TOWNSEND & CO.,)
NO. 46 WALKER STREET.
1861.

C A. ALVORD, PRINTER.

ADDRESS OF HON. JOSEPH HOLT.

Mr. Holt was next introduced to the audience by Hon. Henry Pirtle, who addressed him a few words of welcome.

Then taking the stand, amid prolonged cheers, Mr. Holt spoke as follows:—

Judge Pirtle: I beg you to be assured that I am most thankful for this distinguished and flattering welcome, and for every one of the kind words which have just fallen from your lips, as I am for the hearty response they have received. Spoken by anybody and anywhere, these words would have been cherished by me; but spoken by yourself and in the presence and on behalf of those in whose midst I commenced the battle of life, whose friendship I have ever labored to deserve, and in whose fortunes I have ever felt the liveliest sympathy, they are doubly grateful to my feelings. I take no credit to myself for loving and being faithful to such a government as this, or for uttering, as I do, with every throb of my existence, a prayer for its preservation. In regard to my official conduct, to which you have alluded with such earnest and generous commendation, I must say that no merit can be accorded to me beyond that of having humbly but sincerely struggled to perform a public duty, amid embarrassments which the world can never fully know. In reviewing what is past, I have and shall ever have a bitter sorrow, that, while I was enabled to accomplish so little in behalf of our betrayed and suffering country, others were enabled to accomplish so much against it. You do me exceeding honor in associating me in your remembrance with the hero of Fort Sumter. There is about his name an atmosphere of light that can never grow dim. Surrounded with his little band, by batteries of treason and by infuriated thousands of traitors, the fires upon the altar of patriotism at which he ministered, only waxed the brighter for the gloom that enveloped him, and history will never forget that it was from these fires that was kindled that conflagration that now blazes throughout the length and breadth of the land. Brave among the bravest, incorruptible and unconquerable in his loyalty, amid all the perplexities and trials and sore humiliations that beset him, he well deserves that exalted position in the affections and confidence of the people that he now enjoys; and while none have had better opportunities of knowing this than myself, so I am sure that none could have a prouder joy in bearing testimony to it than I have to-night.

FELLOW-CITIZENS: A few weeks since, in another form, I ventured freely to express my views upon those tragic events which have brought sorrow to every hearthstone and to every heart in our distracted country, and it is not my purpose on this occasion to repeat those views, or to engage in any extended discussion of the questions then examined. It is not necessary that I should do so, since the argument is exhausted, and the popular mind is perfectly familiar with it in all its bearings. I will, however, with your permission, submit a few brief observations upon the absorbing topics of the day, and if I do so with an earnestness and emphasis due alike to the sincerity of my convictions and to the magnitude of the interests involved, it is trusted that none will be offended, not even those who may most widely differ from me.

Could one, an entire stranger to our history, now look down upon the South, and see there a hundred or a hundred and fifty thousand men marching in hostile array, threatening the capture of the capital and the dismemberment of the territory of the republic; and could he look again and see that this army is marshalled and directed by officers recently occupying distinguished places in the civil and military service of the country; and further that the states from which this army has been drawn appear to be one vast, seething cauldron of ferocious passion, he would very naturally conclude that the government of the United States had committed some great crime against its people, and that this uprising was in resistance to wrong and outrages which had been borne until endurance was no longer possible. And yet no conclusion could be further from the truth than this. The government of the United States has been faithful to all its constitutional obligations. For eighty years it has maintained the national honor at home and abroad, and by its prowess, its wisdom, and its justice, has given to the title of an American citizen an elevation among the nations of the earth which the citizens of no republic has enjoyed since Rome was mistress of the world. Under its administration the national domain has stretched away to the Pacific, and that constellation which announced our birth as a people, has expanded from thirteen to thirty-four stars, all, until recently, moving undisturbed and undimmed in their orbs of light and grandeur. The rights of no states have been invaded; no man's property has been despoiled, no man's liberty abridged, no man's life oppressively jeopardized by the action of this government. Under its benign influences the rills of public and private prosperity have swelled into rivulets, and from rivulets into rivers ever brimming in their fullness, and everywhere, and at all periods of its history, its ministrations have fallen as gently on the people of the United States as do the dews of a Summer's night on the flowers and grass of the gardens and fields.

Whence, then, this revolutionary outbreak? Whence the secret spring of this gigantic conspiracy, which, like some huge boa, had completely coiled itself around the limbs and body of the republic, before a single hand was lifted to resist it? Strange, and indeed startling, as the announcement must appear when it falls on the ears of the next generation, the national tragedy, in whose shadow we stand to-night, has come upon us because, in November last, JOHN C. BRECKINRIDGE was not elected President of the United States, and ABRAHAM LINCOLN was. This is the whole story. And I would pray now to know on what was JOHN C. BRECKINRIDGE fed that he has grown so great, that a republic founded by WASHINGTON and cemented by the best blood that has ever coursed in human veins, is to be overthrown because, forsooth, he cannot be its President? Had he been chosen we well know that we should not have heard of this rebellion, for the lever with which it is being moved would have been wanting to the hands of the conspirators. Even after his defeat, could it have been guaranteed, beyond all peradventure, that JEFF. DAVIS, or some other kindred spirit, would be the successor of Mr. LINCOLN, I presume we hazard nothing in assuming that this atrocious movement against the government would not have been set on foot. So much for the principle involved in it. This great crime, then, with which we are grappling, sprang from that "sin by which the angels fell"—an unmastered and profligate ambition—an ambition that "would rather reign in hell than serve in heaven"—that would rather rule supremely over a shattered fragment of the republic than run the chances of sharing with others the honors of the whole.

The conspirators of the South read in the election of Mr. LINCOLN a declaration that the Democratic party had been prostrated, if not finally destroyed, by the selfish intrigues and corruptions of its leaders; they read, too, that the vicious, emaciated, and spavined hobby of the slavery agitation, on which they had so often rode into power, could no longer carry them beyond a given geographical line of our territory, and that in truth this factious and treasonable agitation, on which so many of them had grown great by debauching and denationalizing the mind of a people naturally generous and patriotic, had run its course, and hence, that from the national disgust for this demagogueing, and for the inexorable law of population, the time had come when all those who had no other political capital than this, would have to prepare for retirement to private life, so far at least as the highest offices of the country were concerned. Under the influence of these grim discouragements they resolved to consummate at once—what our political history shows to have been a long-cherished purpose—the dismemberment of the government. They said to themselves: "Since we can no longer monopolize the great offices of the republic as we have been accustomed to do, we will destroy it and build upon its ruins an empire that shall be all our own, and whose spoils neither the North nor the East nor the West shall share with us." Deplorable and humiliating as this certainly is, it is but a rehearsal of the sad, sad story of the past. We had, indeed, supposed that under our Christian civilization we had reached a point in human progress, when a republic could exist without having its life sought by its own offspring; but the Catilines of the South have proved that we were mistaken. Let no man imagine that because this rebellion has been made by men renowned in our civil and military history, that it is, therefore, the less guilty or the less courageously to be resisted. It is precisely this class of men who have subverted the best governments that have ever existed. The purest spirits that have lived in the tide of times, the noblest institutions that have arisen to bless our race, have found among those in whom they had most confided, and whom they had most honored, men wicked enough, either secretly to betray them unto death, or openly to seek their overthrow by lawless violence. The republic of England had its Monk; the republic of France had its BONAPARTE; the republic of Rome had its CÆSAR and its CATILINE, and the Saviour of the world had his Judas Iscariot. It cannot be necessary that I should declare to you, for you know them well, who they are whose parricidal swords are now unsheathed against the republic of the United States. Their names are inscribed upon a scroll of infamy that can never perish. The most distinguished of them were educated by the charity of the government on which they are now making war. For long years they were fed from its table, and clothed from its wardrobe, and had their brows garlanded by its honors. They are the ungrateful sons of a fond mother, who dandled them upon her knee, who lavished upon them the gushing love of her noble and devoted nature, and who nurtured them from the very bosom of her life; and now, in the frenzied excesses of a licentious and baffled ambition, they are stabbing at that bosom with the ferocity with which the tiger springs upon his prey. The President of the United States is heroically and patriotically struggling to baffle the machinations of these most wicked men. I have unbounded gratification in knowing that he has the courage to look traitors in the face, and that, in discharging the duties of his great office, he takes no counsel of his fears. He is entitled to the zealous support of the whole country, and, may I not add without offence, that he will receive the support of all who justly appreciate the boundless blessings of our free institutions?

If this rebellion succeeds it will involve necessarily the destruction of our nationality, the division of our territory, the permanent disruption of the republic. It must rapidly dry up the sources of our material prosperity, and year by year we shall grow more and more impoverished, more and more revolutionary, enfeebled, and debased. Each returning election will bring with it grounds for new civil commotions, and traitors, prepared to strike at the country that has rejected their claims to power, will spring up on every side. Disunion once begun will go on and on indefinitely, and under the influence of the fatal doctrine of secession, not only will states secede from states, but counties will secede from states also, and towns and cities from counties, until universal anarchy will be consummated in each individual who can make good his position by force of arms, claiming the right to defy the power of the government. Thus we should have brought back to us the days of the robber barons with their moated castles and marauding retainers. This doctrine when analyzed is simply a declaration that no physical force shall ever be employed in executing the laws or upholding the government, and a government into whose practical administration such a principle has been introduced, could no more continue to exist than a man could live with an angered cobra in his bosom. If you would know what are the legitimate fruits of secession, look at Virginia and Tennessee, which have so lately given themselves up to the embrace of this monster. There the schools are deserted; the courts of justice closed; public and private credit destroyed; commerce annihilated, debts repudiated; confiscations and spoliations everywhere prevailing; every cheek blanched with fear, and every heart frozen with despair; and all over that desolated land the hand of infuriated passion and crime is waving, with a vulture's scream for blood, the sword of civil war. And this is the Pandemonium which some would have transferred to Kentucky.

But I am not here to discuss this proposition to-night. I wish solemnly to declare before you and the world, that I am for this Union without conditions, one and indivisible, now and forever. I am for its preservation at any and every cost of blood and treasure against all its assailants. I know no neutrality between my country and its foes, whether they be foreign or domestic; no neutrality between that glorious flag which now floats over us, and the ingrates and traitors who would trample it in the dust. My prayer is for victory, complete, enduring and overwhelming, to the armies of the republic over all its enemies. I am against any and every compromise that may be proposed to be made under the guns of the rebels, while, at the same time, I am decidedly in favor of affording every reasonable guarantee for the safety of Southern institutions, which the honest convictions of the people—not the conspirators—of the South may demand, *whenever they shall lay down their arms, but not until then.* The arbitrament of the sword has been defiantly thrust into the face of the government and country, and there is no honorable escape from it. All guarantees and all attempts at adjustment by amendments to the constitution are now scornfully rejected, and the leaders of the rebellion openly proclaim that they are fighting for their independence. In this contemptuous rejection of guarantees, and in this avowal of the objects of the rebellion now so audaciously made, we have a complete exposure of that fraud which, through the slavery agitation, has been practised upon the public credulity for the last fifteen or twenty years. In the light of this revelation, we feel as one awakened from the suffocating tortures of a nightmare, and realize what a baseless dream our apprehensions have been, and of what a traitorous swindle we have been made the victims. They are fighting for their independence! Independence of what? Independence of those laws which they themselves have aided in enacting; independence of that constitution which their fathers framed and to which they are parties and subject by inheritance; independence of that beneficent government on whose treasury and honors they have grown strong and illustrious. When a man commits a robbery on the highway, or a murder in the dark, he thereby declares his independence of the laws under which he lives, and of the society of which he is a member. Should he, when arraigned, avow and justify the offence, he thereby becomes the advocate of the independence he has thus declared; and, if he resists by force of arms the officer, when dragging him to the prison, the penitentiary, or the gallows, he is thereby fighting for the independence he has thus declared and advocated; and such is the condition of the conspirators of the South at this moment. It is no longer a question of Southern rights, which have never been violated, nor of security of Southern institutions, which we know perfectly well have never been interfered with by the general government, but it is purely with us a question of national existence. In meeting this terrible issue which rebellion has made up with the loyal men of the country, we stand upon ground infinitely above all party lines and party platforms—ground as sublime as that on which our fathers stood when they fought the battles of the revolution. I am for throwing into the contest thus forced upon us all the material and moral resources and energies of the nation, in order that the struggle may be brief and as little sanguinary as possible. It is hoped that we shall soon see in the field half a million of patriotic volunteers, marching in columns which will be perfectly irresistible, and, borne in their hands—for no purpose of conquest or subjugation, but of protection only—we may expect within nine months to see the stars and stripes floating in every Southern breeze, and hear going up, wild as the storm, the exultant shout of that emancipated people over their deliverance from the revolutionary terror and despotism, by which they are now tormented and oppressed. The war, conducted on such a scale, will not cost exceeding four or five hundred millions of dollars; and none need be startled at the vastness of this expenditure. The debt thus created will press but slightly upon us; it will be paid and gladly paid by posterity, who will make the best bargain which has been made since the world began, if they can secure to themselves, in its integrity and blessings, such a government as this, at such a cost. But, if in this anticipation we are doomed to disappointment; if the people of the United States have already become so degenerate —may I not say so craven—in the presence of their foes as to surrender up this republic to be dismembered and subverted by the traitors who have reared the standard of revolt against it, then, I trust, the volume of American history will be closed and sealed up forever, and that those who shall survive this national humiliation will take unto themselves some other name, —some name having no relation to the past, no relation to our great ancestors, no relation to those monuments and battle-fields which commemorate alike their heroism, their loyalty, and their glory.

But with the curled lip of scorn we are told by the disunionists that in thus supporting a Republican administration in its endeavors to uphold the constitution and the laws, we are "submissionists," and when they have pronounced this word, they suppose they have imputed to us the sum of all human abasement. Well, let it be confessed; we are "submissionists," and weak and spiritless as it may be deemed by some, we glory in the position we occupy. For example: the law says, "Thou shalt not steal;" we submit to this law, and would not for the world's worth rob our neighbor of his forts, his arsenals, his arms, his munitions of war, his hospital stores, or any thing that is his. Indeed, so impressed are we with the obligations of this law, that we would no more think of plundering from our neighbor half a million of dollars because found in his unprotected mints, than we would think of filching a purse from his pocket in a crowded thoroughfare. Write us down, therefore, "submissionists." Again: the law says, "Thou shalt not swear falsely;" we submit to this law, and while in the civil or military service of the country, with an oath to support the constitution of the United States resting upon our consciences, we would not for any earthly consideration engage in the formation or execution of a conspiracy to subvert that very constitution, and with it the government to which it has given birth. Write us down, therefore, again, "submissionists." Yet again: when a President has been elected in strict accordance with the form and spirit of the constitution, and has been regularly installed into office, and is honestly striving to discharge his duty by snatching the republic from the jaws of a gigantic treason which threatens to crush it, we care not what his name may or may not be, or what the designation of his political party, or what the platform on which he stood during the presidential canvass; we believe we fulfil in the sight of earth and heaven our highest obligations to our country, in giving to him an earnest and loyal support in the struggle in which he is engaged.

Nor are we at all disturbed by the flippant taunt that in thus submitting to the authority of our government we are necessarily cowards. We know whence this taunt comes, and we estimate it at its true value. We hold that there is a higher courage in the performance of duty than in the commission of crime. The tiger of the jungle and the cannibal of the South Sea Islands have that courage in which the revolutionists of the day make their especial boast; the angels of God and the spirits of just men made perfect have had, and have that courage which submits to the laws. Lucifer was a non-submissionist, and the first secessionist of whom history has given us any account, and the chains which he wears fitly, express the fate due to all who openly defy the laws of their Creator and of their country. He rebelled because the Almighty would not yield to him the throne of heaven. The principle of the Southern rebellion is the same. Indeed, in this submission to the laws is found the chief distinction between good men and devils. A good man obeys the laws of truth, of honesty, of morality, and all those laws which have been enacted by competent authority for the government and protection of the country in which he lives; a devil obeys only his own ferocious and profligate passions. The principle on which this rebellion proceeds, that laws have in themselves no sanctions, no binding force upon the conscience, and that every man, under the promptings of interest, or passion, or caprice, may, at will, and honorably too, strike at the government that shelters him, is one of utter demoralization, and should be trodden out as you would tread on a spark that has fallen on the roof of your dwelling. Its unchecked prevalence would resolve society into chaos, and leave you without the slightest guarantee for life, liberty, or property. It is time that, in their majesty, the people of the United States should make known to the world that this government, in its dignity and power, is something more than a moot court, and that the citizen who makes war upon it is a traitor, not only in theory but in fact, and should have meted out to him a traitor's doom. The country wants no bloody sacrifice, but it must and will have peace, cost what it may.

Before closing, I desire to say a few words on the relations of Kentucky to the pending rebellion; and as we are all Kentuckians here together to-night, and as this is purely a family matter, which concerns the honor of us all, I hope we may be permitted to speak to each other upon it with entire freedom. I shall not detain you with observations on the hostile and defiant position assumed by the governor of your state. In his reply to the requisition made upon him for volunteers under the proclamation of the President, he has, in my judgment, written and finished his own history, his epitaph included, and it is probable that in future the world will little concern itself as to what his excellency may propose to do, or as to what he may propose not to do. That response has made for Kentucky a record that has already brought a burning blush to the cheek of many of her sons, and is destined to bring it to the cheek of many more in the years which are to come. It is a shame, indeed a crying shame, that a state with so illustrious a past should have written for her, by her own chief magistrate, a page of history so utterly humiliating as this. But your legislature have determined that during the present unhappy war the attitude of the state shall be that of strict neutrality, and it is upon this determination that I wish respectfully but frankly to comment. As the motives which governed the legislature were doubtless patriotic and conservative, the conclusion arrived at cannot be condemned as dishonorable; still, in view of the manifest duty of the state and of possible results, I cannot but regard it as mistaken and false, and one which may have fatal consequences. Strictly and legally speaking, Kentucky must go out of the Union before she can be neutral. Within it she is necessarily either faithful to the government of the United States, or she is disloyal to it. If this crutch of neutrality, upon which her well-meaning but ill-judging politicians are halting, can find any middle ground on which to rest, it has escaped my researches, though I have diligently sought it. Neutrality, in the sense of those who now use the term, however patriotically designed, is, in effect, but a snake in the grass of rebellion, and those who handle it will sooner or later feel its fangs. Said one who spake as never man spake, "He who is not with us is against us;" and of none of the conflicts which have arisen between men or between nations, could this be more truthfully said than of that in which we are now involved. Neutrality necessarily implies indifference. Is Kentucky indifferent to the issue of this contest? Has she, indeed, nothing at stake? Has she no compact with her sister states to keep, no plighted faith to uphold, no renown to sustain, no glory to win? Has she no horror of that crime of crimes now being committed against us by that stupendous rebellion which has arisen like a tempest-cloud in the South? We rejoice to know that she is still a member of this Union, and as such she has the same interest in resisting this rebellion that each limb of the body has in resisting a poignard whose point is aimed at the heart. It is her house that is on fire; has she no interest in extinguishing the conflagration? Will she stand aloof and announce herself neutral between the raging flames and the brave men who are periling their lives to subdue them? Hundreds of thousands of citizens of other states—men of culture and character, of thought and of toil—men who have a deep stake in life, and an intense appreciation of its duties and responsibilities, who know the worth of this blessed government of ours, and do not prize even their own blood above it—I say, hundreds of thousands of such men have left their homes, their workshops, their offices, their counting-houses, and their fields, and are now rallying about our flag, freely offering their all to sustain it, and since the days that crusading Europe threw its hosts upon the embattled plains of Asia, no deeper, or more earnest, or grander spirit has stirred the souls of men than that which now sways those mighty masses whose gleaming banners are destined ere long to make bright again the earth and sky of the distracted South. Can Kentucky look upon this sublime spectacle of patriotism unmoved, and then say to herself: "I will spend neither blood nor treasure, but I will shrink away while the battle rages, and after it has been fought and won, I will return to the camp, well assured that if I cannot claim the laurels, I will at least enjoy the blessings of the victory?" Is this all that remains of her chivalry—of the chivalry of the land of the Shelbys, the Johnsons, the Allens, the Clays, the Adairs, and the Davises? Is there a Kentuckian within the sound of my voice to-night, who can hear the anguished cry of his country as she wrestles and writhes in the olds of this gigantic treason, and then lay himself down upon his pillow with this thought of neutrality, without feeling that he has something in his bosom which stings him worse than would an adder? Have we, within the brief period of eighty years, descended so far from the mountain heights on which our fathers stood, that already, in our degeneracy, we proclaim our blood too precious, our treasure too valuable to be devoted to the preservation of such a government as this? They fought through a seven years' war, with the greatest power on earth, for the hope, the bare hope, of being able to found this republic, and now that it is no longer a hope nor an experiment, but a glorious reality, which has excited the admiration and the homage of the nations, and has covered us with blessings as "the waters cover the channels of the sea," have we, their children, no years of toil, of sacrifice, and of battle even, if need be, to give, to save it from absolute destruction at the hands of men who, steeped in guilt, are perpetrating against us and humanity a crime, for which I verily believe the blackest page of the history of the world's darkest period furnishes no parallel? Can it be possible that in the history of the American people we have already reached a point of degeneracy so low, that the work of WASHINGTON and FRANKLIN, of ADAMS and JEFFERSON, of HANCOCK and HENRY, is to be overthrown by the morally begrimed and pigmied conspirators who are now tugging at its foundations? It would be the overturning of the Andes by the miserable reptiles that are crawling in the sands at their base.

But our neutral fellow-citizens in the tenderness of their hearts say: "This effusion of blood sickens us." Then do all in your power to bring it to an end. Let the whole strength of this commonwealth be put forth in support of the government, in order that the war may be terminated by a prompt suppression of the rebellion. The longer the struggle continues, the fiercer will be its spirit, and the more fearful the waste of life attending it. You therefore only aggravate the calamity you deplore by standing aloof from the combat. But again they say, "we cannot fight our brethren." Indeed. But your brethren can fight you, and with a good will, too. Wickedly and wantonly have they commenced this war against you and your institutions, and ferociously are they prosecuting it. They take no account of the fact that the massacre with which they hope their swords will, ere long, be clogged, must be the massacre of their brethren. However much we may bow our heads at the confession, it is nevertheless true that every free people that have existed have been obliged, at one period or other of their history, to fight for their liberties against traitors within their own bosoms, and that people who have not the greatness of soul thus to fight, cannot long continue to be free, nor do they deserve to be so.

There is not, and there cannot be, any neutral ground for a loyal people between their own government and those who, at the head of armies, are menacing its destruction. Your inaction is not neutrality, though you may delude yourselves with the belief that it is so. With this rebellion confronting you, when you refuse to co-operate actively with your government in subduing it, you thereby condemn the government, and assume towards it an attitude of antagonism. Your inaction is a virtual indorsement of the rebellion, and if you do not thereby give to the rebels precisely that "aid and comfort" spoken of in the constitution, you certainly afford them a most powerful encouragement and support. That they regard your present position as friendly to them, is proved by the fact that, in a recent enactment of the Confederate Congress confiscating the debts due from their own citizens to those of loyal states, the debts due to the people of Kentucky are expressly excepted. Is not this significant? Does it leave any room for doubt that the Confederate Congress suppose they have discovered, under the guise of your neutrality, a lurking sympathy for their cause which entitles you to be treated as friends, if not as active allies? Patriotic as was the purpose of her apprehensive statesmen in placing her in the anomalous position she now occupies, it cannot be denied that Kentucky by her present attitude is exerting a potent influence in strengthening the rebellion, and is, therefore, false alike to her loyalty and to her fame. You may rest well assured that this estimate of your neutrality is entertained by the true men of the country in all the states which are now sustaining the government. Within the last few weeks how many of those gallant volunteers who have left home and kindred and all that is dear to them, and are now under a Southern sun, exposing themselves to death from disease and to death from battle, and are accounting their lives as nothing in the effort they are making for the deliverance of your government and theirs; how many of them have said to me in sadness and in longing, "Will not Kentucky help me?" How my soul would have leaped could I have answered promptly, confidently, exultingly, "Yes, she will." But when I thought of this neutrality my heart sank within me, and I did not and I could not look those brave men in the face. And yet I could not answer, "No." I could not crush myself to the earth under the self-abasement of such a reply. I therefore said—and may my country sustain me—"I hope, I trust, I pray, nay, I believe Kentucky will yet do her duty."

If this government is to be destroyed, ask yourselves are you willing it shall be recorded in history that Kentucky stood by in the greatness of her strength and lifted not a hand to stay the catastrophe? If it is to be saved, as I verily believe it is, are you willing it shall be written that, in the immeasurable glory which must attend the achievement, Kentucky had no part?

I will only add, if Kentucky wishes the waters of her beautiful Ohio to be dyed in blood—if she wishes her harvest fields, now waving in their abundance, to be trampled beneath the feet of hostile soldiery, as a flower-garden is trampled beneath the threshings of the tempest—if she wishes the homes where her loved ones are now gathered in peace, invaded by the proscriptive fury of a military despotism, sparing neither life nor property—if she wishes the streets of her towns and cities grown with grass, and the steamboats of her rivers to lie rotting at her wharves, then let her join the Southern Confederacy; but if she would have the bright waters of that river flow on in their gladness—if she would have her harvests peacefully gathered to her garners—if she would have the lullabies of her cradles and the songs of her homes uninvaded by the cries and terrors of battle—if she would have the streets of her towns and cities again filled with the hum and throngs of busy trade, and her rivers and her shores once more vocal with the steamer's whistle, that anthem of a free and prosperous commerce, then let her stand fast by the stars and stripes, and do her duty and her whole duty as a member of this Union. Let her brave people say to the President of the United States: "You are our chief magistrate; the government you have in charge, and are striving to save from dishonor and dismemberment, is our government; your cause is indeed our cause; your battles are our battles; make room for us, therefore, in the ranks of your armies, that your triumph may be our triumph also."

Even as with the Father of us all I would plead for salvation, so, my countrymen, as upon my very knees, would I plead with you for the life, aye for the life, of our great and beneficent institutions. But if the traitor's knife, now at the throat of the republic, is to do its work, and this government is fated to add yet another to that long line of sepulchres which whiten the highway of the past, then my heartfelt prayer to God is, that it may be written in history, that the blood of its life was not found upon the skirts of Kentucky.

LETTER OF HON. JOSEPH HOLT.

WASHINGTON, *Friday*, *May* 31, 1861.

J. F. SPEED, Esq.

My Dear Sir: The recent overwhelming vote in favor of the Union in Kentucky has afforded unspeakable gratification to all true men throughout the country. That vote indicates that the people of that gallant state have been neither seduced by the arts nor terrified by the menaces of the revolutionists in their midst, and that it is their fixed purpose to remain faithful to a government which, for nearly seventy years, has remained faithful to them. Still it cannot be denied that there is in the bosom of that state a band of agitators, who, though few in number, are yet powerful from the public confidence they have enjoyed, and who have been, and doubtless will continue to be, unceasing in their endeavor to force Kentucky to unite her fortunes with those of the rebel Confederacy of the South. In view of this and of the well-known fact that several of the seceded states have by fraud and violence been driven to occupy their present false and fatal position, I cannot, even with the encouragement of her late vote before me, look upon the political future of our native state without a painful solicitude. Never have the safety and honor of her people required the exercise of so much vigilance and of so much courage on their part. If true to themselves, the stars and stripes, which, like angel's wings, have so long guarded their homes from every oppression, will still be theirs; but if, chasing the dreams of men's ambition, they shall prove false, the blackness of darkness can but faintly predict the gloom that awaits them. The legislature, it seems, has determined by resolution that the state, pending the present unhappy war, shall occupy neutral ground. *I must say, in all frankness, and without desiring to reflect upon the course or sentiments of any, that, in this struggle for the existence of our government, I can neither practise nor profess nor feel neutrality. I would as soon think of being neutral in a contest between an officer of justice and an incendiary arrested in an attempt to fire the dwelling over my head; for the government whose overthrow is sought, is for me the shelter not only of home, kindred and friends, but of every earthly blessing which I can hope to enjoy on this side of the grave.* If, however, from a natural horror of fratricidal strife, or from her intimate social and business relations with the South, Kentucky shall determine to maintain the neutral attitude assumed for her by her legislature, her position will still be an honorable one, though falling far short of that full measure of loyalty which her history has so constantly illustrated. Her executive, ignoring, as I am happy to believe, alike the popular and legislative sentiment of the state, has, by proclamation, forbidden the government of the United States from marching troops across her territory. This is in no sense a neutral step, but one of aggressive hostility. The troops of the Federal Government have as clear a constitutional right to pass over the soil of Kentucky as they have to march along the streets of Washington; and could this prohibition be effective, it would not only be a violation of the fundamental law, but would, in all its tendencies, be directly in advancement of the revolution, and might, in an emergency easily imagined, compromise the highest national interests. I was rejoiced that the legislature so promptly refused to endorse this proclamation as expressive of the true policy of the state. But I turn away from even this to the ballot-box, and find an abounding consolation in the conviction it inspires, that the popular heart of Kentucky, in its devotion to the Union, is far in advance alike of legislative resolve and executive proclamation.

But as it is well understood that the late popular demonstration has rather scotched than killed rebellion in Kentucky, I propose inquiring, as briefly as practicable, whether in the recent action or present declared policy of the administration, or in the history of the pending revolution, or in the objects it seeks to accomplish, or in the results which must follow from it, if successful, there can be discovered any reasons why that state should sever the ties that unite her with a Confederacy in whose councils and upon whose battle-fields she has won so much fame, and under whose protection she has enjoyed so much prosperity.

For more than a month after the inauguration of President LINCOLN, the manifestations seemed unequivocal that his administration would seek a peaceful solution of our unhappy political troubles, and would look to time and amendments of the Federal Constitution, adopted in accordance with its provisions, to bring back the revolted states to their allegiance. So marked was the effect of these manifestations in tranquilizing the border states and in reassuring their loyalty, that the conspirators who had set this revolution on foot took the alarm. *While affecting to despise these states as not sufficiently intensified in their devotion to African servitude, they knew they could never succeed in their treasonable enterprise without their support. Hence it was resolved to precipitate a collision of arms with the federal authorities, in the hope that under the panic and exasperation incident to the commencement of a civil war, the border states, following the natural bent of their sympathies, would array themselves against the government.* Fort Sumter, occupied by a feeble garrison, and girdled by powerful if not impregnable batteries, afforded convenient means for accomplishing their purpose, and for testing also their theory, that blood was needed to cement the new Confederacy. Its provisions were exhausted, and the request made by the President, in the interests of peace and humanity, for the privilege of replenishing its stores, had been refused. The Confederate authorities were aware—for so the gallant commander of the fort had declared to them—that in two days a capitulation from starvation must take place. A peaceful surrender, however, would not have subserved their aims. They sought the clash of arms and the effusion of blood as an instrumentality for impressing the border states, and they sought the humiliation of the government and the dishonor of its flag as a means of giving prestige to their own cause. The result is known. Without the slightest provocation, a heavy cannonade was opened upon the fort, and borne by its helpless garrison for hours without reply; and when, in the progress of the bombardment, the fortification became wrapped in flames, the besieging batteries, in violation of the usages of civilized warfare, instead of relaxing or suspending, redoubled their fires. *A more wanton or wicked war was never commenced on any government whose history has been written.* Contemporary with and following the fall of Sumter, the siege of Fort Pickens was and still is actively pressed; the property of the United States government continued to be seized wherever found, and its troops, by fraud or force, captured in the state of Texas, in violation of a solemn compact with its authorities that they should be permitted to embark without molestation. This was the requital which the Lone Star State made to brave men, who, through long years of peril and privation, had guarded its frontiers against the incursions of the savages. In the midst of the most active and extended warlike preparations in the South, the announcement was made by the Secretary of War of the seceded states, and echoed with taunts and insolent bravadoes by the Southern press, that Washington City was to be invaded and captured, and that the flag of the Confederate States would soon float over the dome of its Capitol. Soon thereafter there followed an invitation to all the world—embracing necessarily the outcasts and desperadoes of every sea—to accept letters of marque and reprisal, to prey upon the rich and unprotected commerce of the United States.

In view of these events and threatenings, what was the duty of the chief magistrate of the republic? He might have taken counsel of the revolutionists and trembled under their menaces; he might, upon the fall of Sumter, have directed that Fort Pickens should be surrendered without firing a gun in its defence, and proceeding yet further, and meeting fully the requirements of the "let us alone" policy insisted on in the South, he might have ordered that the stars and stripes should be laid in the dust in the presence of every bit of rebel bunting that might appear. *But he did none of these things, nor could he have done them without forfeiting his oath and betraying the most sublime trust that has ever been confided to the hands of man.* With a heroic fidelity to his constitutional obligations, feeling justly that these obligations charged him with the protection of the republic and its capital against the assaults alike of foreign and domestic enemies, he threw himself on the loyalty of the country for support in the struggle upon which he was about to enter, and nobly has that appeal been responded to. States containing an aggregate population of nineteen millions have answered to the appeal as with the voice of one man, offering soldiers without number, and treasure without limitation for the service of the government. In these states, fifteen hundred thousand freemen cast their votes in favor of candidates supporting the rights of the South, at the last presidential election, and yet everywhere, alike in popular assemblies and upon the tented field, this million and a half of voters are found yielding to none in the zeal with which they rally to their country's flag. They are not less the friends of the South than before; but they realize that the question now presented is not one of administrative policy, or of the claims of the North, the South, the East, or the West; but is, simply, whether nineteen millions of people shall tamely and ignobly permit five or six millions to overthrow and destroy institutions which are the common property, and have been the common blessings and glory of all. The great thoroughfares of the North, the East, and the West, are luminous with the banners and glistening with the bayonets of citizen soldiers marching to the capital, or to the other points of rendezvous; but they come in no hostile spirit to the South. *If called to press her soil, they will not ruffle a flower of her gardens, nor a blade of grass of her fields in unkindness. No excesses will mark the footsteps of the armies of the republic; no institution of the states will be invaded or tampered with, no rights of persons or of property will be violated. The known purposes of the administration, and the high character of the troops employed, alike guarantee the truthfulness of this statement.* When an insurrection was apprehended a few weeks since in Maryland, the Massachusetts regiment at once offered their services to suppress it. These volunteers have been denounced by the press of the South as "knaves and vagrants," "the dregs and offscourings of the populace," who would "rather filch a handkerchief than fight an enemy in manly combat;" yet we know here that their discipline and bearing are most admirable, and, I presume, it may be safely affirmed, that a larger amount of social position, culture, fortune, and elevation of character, has never been found in so large an army in any age or country. *If they go to the South, it will be as friends and protectors, to relieve the Union sentiment of the seceded states from the cruel domination by which it is oppressed and silenced, to unfurl the stars and stripes in the midst of those who long to look upon them, and to restore the flag that bears them to the forts and arsenals from which disloyal hands have torn it. Their mission will be one of peace, unless wicked and bloodthirsty men shall unsheath the sword across their pathway.*

It is in vain for the revolutionists to exclaim that this is "subjugation." It is so, *precisely in the sense in which you and I and all law-abiding citizens are subjugated.* The people of the South are our brethren, and while we obey the laws enacted by our joint authority, and keep a compact to which we all are parties, we only ask that they shall be required to do the same. We believe that their safety demands this; we know that ours does. We impose no burden which we ourselves do not bear; we claim no privilege or blessing which our brethren of the South shall not equally share. Their country is our country, and ours is theirs; and that unity both of country and of government which the providence of God and the compacts of men have created, we could not ourselves, without self-immolation, destroy, nor can we permit it to be destroyed by others.

Equally vain is it for them to declare that they only wish "to be let alone," and that, in establishing the independence of the seceded states, they do those which remain in the old confederacy no harm. The free states, if allowed the opportunity of doing so, will undoubtedly concede every guarantee needed to afford complete protection to the institutions of the South, and to furnish assurances of her perfect equality in the Union; but all such guarantees and assurances are now openly spurned, and the only Southern right now insisted on is that of dismembering the republic. It is perfectly certain, that in the attempted exercise of this right, neither states nor statesmen will be "let alone." Should a ruffian meet me in the streets, and seek, with his axe, to hew an arm and a leg from my body, I would not the less resist him because, as a dishonored and helpless trunk, I might perchance survive the mutilation. It is easy to perceive what fatal results to the old confederacy would follow, should the blow now struck at its integrity ultimately triumph. We can well understand what degradation it would bring to it abroad, and what weakness at home; what exhaustion from incessant war and standing armies, and from the erection of fortifications along the thousands of miles of new frontiers; what embarrassments to commerce from having its natural channels encumbered or cut off; what elements of disintegration and revolution would be introduced from the pernicious example; and, above all, what humiliation would cover the whole American people for having failed in their great mission to demonstrate before the world the capacity of our race for self-government.

While a far more fearful responsibility has fallen upon President Lincoln than upon any of his predecessors, it must be admitted that he has met it with promptitude and fearlessness. CICERO, in one of his orations against CATILINE, speaking of the credit due himself for having suppressed the conspiracy of that arch-traitor, said, "If the glory of him who founded Rome was great, how much greater should be that of him who had saved it from overthrow, after it had grown to be mistress of the world!" So may it be said of the glory of that statesman or chieftain who shall snatch this republic from the vortex of revolution, now that it has expanded from ocean to ocean—has become the admiration of the world, and has rendered the fountains of the lives of thirty millions of people fountains of happiness.

The vigorous measures adopted for the safety of Washington, and the government itself, may seem open to criticism, in some of their details, to those who have yet to learn that not only has war, like peace, its laws, but that it has also its privileges and its duties. Whatever of severity, or even of irregularity, may have arisen, will find its justification in the pressure of the terrible necessity under which the administration has been called to act. When a man feels the poignard of the destroyer at his bosom, he is not likely to consult the law books as to the mode or measure of his rights of self-defence. What is true of individuals is, in this respect, equally true of governments. *The man who thinks he has become disloyal because of what the administration has done, will probably discover, after a close examination, that he was disloyal before.* But for what has been done, Washington might ere this have been a smouldering heap of ruins.

They have noted the course of public affairs to little advantage who suppose that the election of LINCOLN was the real ground of the revolutionary outbreak that has occurred. The roots of the revolution may be traced back for more than a quarter of a century, and an unholy lust for power is the soil out of which it sprang. A prominent member of the band of agitators declared in one of his speeches at Charleston, last November or December, that they had been occupied for thirty years in the work of severing South Carolina from the Union. When General JACKSON crushed nullification, he said it would revive again under the form of the slavery agitation, and we have lived to see his prediction verified. Indeed, that agitation, during the last fifteen or twenty years, has been almost the entire stock-in-trade of Southern politicians. The Southern people, known to be as generous in their impulses as they are chivalric, were not wrought into a frenzy of passion by the intemperate words of a few fanatical abolitionists; for these words, if left to themselves, would have fallen to the ground as pebbles into the sea, and would have been heard of no more. But it was the echo of those words, repeated with exaggerations for the thousandth time by Southern politicians, in the halls of Congress, and in the deliberative and popular assemblies, and through the press of the South, that produced the exasperation which has proved so potent a lever in the hands of the conspirators. The cloud was fully charged, and the juggling revolutionists who held the wires, and could at will direct its lightnings, appeared at Charleston, broke up the Democratic convention assembled to nominate a candidate for the presidency, and thus secured the election of Mr. LINCOLN. Having thus rendered this certain, they at once set to work to bring the popular mind of the South to the point of determining in advance that the election of a Republican president would be, *per se*, cause for a dissolution of the Union. They were but too successful, and to this result the inaction and indecision of the border states deplorably contributed. When the election of Mr. LINCOLN was announced, there was rejoicing in the streets of Charleston, and doubtless at other points in the South; for it was believed by the conspirators that this had brought a tide in the current of their machinations which would bear them on to victory. The drama of secession was now open, and state after state rapidly rushed out of the Union, and their members withdrew from Congress. The revolution was pressed on with this hot haste in order that no time should be allowed for reaction in the Northern mind, or for any adjustment of the slavery issues by the action of Congress or of the state legislatures. Had the Southern members continued in their seats, a satisfactory compromise would, no doubt, have been arranged and passed before the adjournment of Congress. As it was, after their retirement, and after Congress had become republican, an amendment to the constitution was adopted by a two-thirds vote, declaring that Congress should never interfere with slavery in the states, and declaring, further, that this amendment should be irrevocable. Thus we falsified the clamor so long and so insidiously rung in the ears of the Southern people, that the abolition of slavery in the states was the ultimate aim of the Republican party. But even this amendment, and all others which may be needed to furnish the guarantees demanded, are now defeated by the secession of eleven states, which, claiming to be out of the Union, will refuse to vote upon, and, in effect, will vote against, any proposals to modify the federal constitution. There are now thirty-four states in the confederacy, three-fourths of which, being twenty-six, must concur in the adoption of any amendment before it can become a part of the constitution; but the secession of eleven states leaves but twenty-three whose vote can possibly be secured, which is less than the constitutional number.

Thus we have the extraordinary and discreditable spectacle of a revolution made by certain states, professedly on the ground that guarantees for the safety of their institutions are denied them, and, at the same time, instead of co-operating with their sister states in obtaining these guarantees, they designedly assume a hostile attitude, and thereby render it constitutionally impossible to secure them. This profound dissimulation shows that it was not the safety of the South, but its severance from the confederacy, which was sought from the beginning. Cotemporary with, and in some cases preceding, these acts of secession, the greatest outrages were committed upon the government of the United States by the states engaged in them. Its forts, arsenals, arms, barracks, custom-houses, post-offices, moneys, and, indeed, every species of its property within the limits of these states, were seized and appropriated, down to the very hospital stores for the sick soldiers. More than half a million of dollars was plundered from the mint at New Orleans. United States vessels were received from the defiled hands of their officers in command, and, as if in the hope of consecrating official treachery as one of the public virtues of the age, the surrender of an entire military department by a general, to the keeping of whose honor it had been confided, was deemed worthy of the commendation and thanks of the conventions of several states. All these lawless proceedings were well understood to have been prompted and directed by men occupying seats in the capitol, some of whom were frank enough to declare that they could not and would not, though in a minority, live under a government which they could not control. In this declaration is found the key which unlocks the whole of the complicated machinery of this revolution. The profligate ambition of public men in all ages and lands has been the rock on which republics have been split. Such men have arisen in our midst—men who, because unable permanently to grasp the helm of the ship, are willing to destroy it in the hope to command some one of the rafts that may float away from the wreck. The effect is to degrade us to a level with the military bandits of Mexico and South America, who, when beaten at an election, fly to arms, and seek to master by the sword what they have been unable to control by the ballot-box.

The atrocious acts enumerated were acts of war, and might all have been treated as such by the late administration; but the President patriotically cultivated peace—how anxiously and how patiently the country well knows. *While, however, the revolutionary leaders greeted him with all hails to his face, they did not the less diligently continue to whet their swords behind his back. Immense military preparations were made, so that when the moment for striking at the government of the United States arrived, the revolutionary states leaped into the contest clad in full armor.*

As if nothing should be wanting to darken this page of history, the seceded States have already entered upon the work of confiscating the debts due from their citizens to the North and North-west. The millions thus gained will doubtless prove a pleasant substitute for those guarantees now so scornfully rejected. To these confiscations will probably succeed soon those of lands and negroes owned by citizens of loyal states; and, indeed, the apprehension of this step is already sadly disturbing the fidelity of non-resident proprietors. Fortunately, however, infirmity of faith, springing from such a cause, is not likely to be contagious. *The war begun is being prosecuted by the Confederate States in a temper as fierce and unsparing as that which characterizes conflicts between the most hostile nations. Letters of marque and reprisals are being granted* to all who seek them, so that our coasts will soon swarm with these piratical cruisers, as the President has properly denounced them. Every buccaneer who desires to rob American commerce upon the ocean, can, for the asking, obtain a warrant to do so, in the name of the new republic. To crown all, large bodies of Indians have been mustered into the service of the revolutionary states, and are now conspicuous in the ranks of the Southern army. A leading North Carolina journal, noting their stalwart frames and unerring markmanship, observes, with an exultation positively fiendish, that they are armed, not only with the rifle, but also with *the scalping-knife and tomahawk.*

Is Kentucky willing to link her name in history with the excesses and crimes which have sullied this revolution at every step of its progress? Can she soil her pure hands with its booty? She possesses the noblest heritage that God has granted to his children; is she prepared to barter it away for that miserable mess of pottage which the gratification of the unholy ambition of her public men would bring to her lips? Can she, without laying her face in the very dust for shame, become a participant in the spoliation of the commerce of her neighbors and friends, by contributing her star, hitherto so stainless in its glory, to light the corsair on his way? Has the warwhoop which used to startle the sleep of our frontiers, so died away in her ears that she is willing to take the red-handed savage to her bosom as the champion of her rights and the representative of her spirit? Must she not first forget her own heroic sons, who perished, butchered and scalped, upon the disastrous field of Raisin?

The object of the revolution, as avowed by all who are pressing it forward is the permanent dismemberment of the Confederacy. The dream of reconstruction—used during the last winter as a lure to draw the hesitating or the hopeful into the movement—has been formally abandoned. If Kentucky separates herself from the Union, it must be upon the basis that the separation is to be final and eternal. Is there aught in the organization or administration of the government of the United States to justify, on her part, an act so solemn and so perilous? Could the wisest of her lawyers, if called upon, find material for an indictment in any or in all the pages of the history of the republic? Could the most leprous-lipped of its calumniators point to a single state or territory, or community or citizen, that it has wronged or oppressed? It would be impossible. *So far as the slave states are concerned, their protection has been complete, and if it has not been, it has been the fault of their statesmen, who have had the control of the government since its foundation.*

The census returns show that during the year 1860, the fugitive slave law was executed more faithfully and successfully than it had been during the preceding ten years. Since the installation of President Lincoln, not a case has arisen in which the fugitive has not been returned, and that, too, without any opposition from the people. Indeed, the fidelity with which it was understood to be the policy of the administration to enforce the provisions of this law, has caused a perfect panic among the runaway slaves in the free states, and they have been escaping in multitudes to Canada, unpursued and unreclaimed by their masters. Is there found in this, reason for a dissolution of the Union?

That the slave states are not recognized as equals in the Confederacy, has for several years been the cry of demagogues and conspirators. But what is the truth? Not only according to the theory, but the actual practice of the government, the slave states have ever been, and still are, in all respects, the peers of the free. Of the fourteen presidents who have been elected, seven were citizens of slave states, and of the seven remaining, three represented Southern principles, and received the votes of the Southern people; so that, in our whole history, but four presidents have been chosen who can be claimed as the special champions of the policy and principles of the free states, and even these so only in a modified sense. Does this look as if the South had ever been deprived of her equal share of the honors and powers of the government? The Supreme Court has decided that the citizens of the slave states can, at will, take their slaves into all the territories of the United States; and this decision, which has never been resisted or interfered with in a single case, is the law of the land, and the whole power of the government is pledged to enforce it. That it will be loyally enforced by the present administration, I entertain no doubt. A Republican Congress, at the late session, organized three new territories, and in the organic law of neither was there introduced or attempted to be introduced, the slightest restriction upon the rights of the Southern emigrant to bring his slaves with him. At this moment, therefore, and I state it without qualification, there is not a territory belonging to the United States into which the Southern people may not introduce their slaves at pleasure, and enjoy their complete protection. Kentucky should consider this great and undeniable fact, before which all the frothy rant of demagogues and disunionists must disappear as a bank of fog before the wind. But were it otherwise, and did a defect exist in our organic law, or in the practical administration of the government, in reference to the rights of Southern slaveholders in the territories, still the question would be a mere abstraction, since the laws of climate forbid the establishment of slavery in such a latitude; and to destroy such institutions as ours for such a cause, instead of patiently trying to remove it, would be little short of national insanity. It would be to burn the house down over our heads merely because there is a leak in the roof; to scuttle the ship in mid-ocean merely because there is a difference of opinion among the crew as to the point of the compass to which the vessel should be steered; it would be, in fact, to apply the knife to the throat instead of to the cancer of the patient.

But what remains? Though, say the disunionists, the Fugitive Slave law is honestly enforced, and though, under the shelter of the Supreme Court, we can take our slaves into the territories, the Northern people will persist in discussing the institution of slavery, and therefore we will break up the government. It is true that slavery has been very intemperately discussed in the North, and it is equally true that until we have an Asiatic despotism, crushing out all freedom of speech and of the press, this discussion will probably continue. In this age and country all institutions, human and divine, are discussed, and so they ought to be; and all that cannot bear discussion must go to the wall, where they ought to go. It is not pretended, however, that the discussion of slavery, which has been continued in our country for more than forty years, has in any manner disturbed or weakened the foundation of the institution. On the contrary, we learn from the press of the seceded states that their slaves were never more tranquil or obedient. There are zealots—happily few in number—both North and South, whose language upon this question is alike extravagant and alike deserving our condemnation. Those who assert that slavery should be extirpated by the sword, and those who maintain that the great mission of the white man upon earth is to enslave the black, are not far apart in the folly and atrocity of their sentiments.

Before proceeding further, Kentucky should measure well the depth of the gulf she is approaching, and look well to the feet of her guides. Before forsaking a Union in which her people have enjoyed such uninterrupted and such boundless prosperity, she should ask herself, not once, but many times, why do I go, and where am I going? In view of what has been said, it would be difficult to answer the first branch of the inquiry, but to answer the second part is patent to all, as are the consequences which would follow the movement. In giving her great material and moral resources to the support of the Southern Confederacy, Kentucky might prolong the desolating struggle that rebellious states are making to overthrow a government which they have only known in its blessings; but the triumph of the government would nevertheless be certain in the end. *She would abandon a government strong and able to protect her, for one that is weak, and that contains, in the very elements of its life, the seeds of distraction and early dissolution. She would adopt, as the law of her existence, the right of secession—a right which has no foundation in jurisprudence, or logic, or in our political history; which Madison, the father of the federal constitution, denounced; which has been denounced by most of the states and prominent statesmen now insisting upon its exercise; which, in introducing a principle of indefinite disintegration, cuts up all confederate governments by the roots, and gives them over a prey to the caprices, and passions, and transient interests of their members, as autumnal leaves are given to the winds which blow upon them.* In 1814, the *Richmond Enquirer*, then, as now, the organ of public opinion in the South, pronounced secession to be treason, and nothing else, and such was then the doctrine of Southern statesmen. What was true then is equally true now. The prevalence of this pernicious heresy is mainly the fruit of that farce called "state rights," which demagogues have been so long playing under tragic mask, and which has done more than all things else to unsettle the foundations of the republic, by estranging the people from the federal government, as one to be distrusted and resisted, instead of being, what it is, emphatically their own creation, at all times obedient to their will, and in its ministrations the grandest reflex of the greatness and beneficence of popular power that has ever ennobled the history of our race. Said Mr. Clay: "I owe a supreme allegiance to the general government, and to my state a subordinate one." And this terse language disposes of the whole controversy which has arisen out of the secession movement in regard to the allegiance of the citizen. As the power of the states and federal governnent are in perfect harmony with each other, so there can be no conflict between the allegiance due to them; each, while acting within the sphere of its constitutional authority, is entitled to be obeyed; but when a state, throwing off all constitutional restraints, seeks to destroy the general government, to say that its citizens are bound to follow in its career of crime, and discard the supreme allegiance they owe to the government assailed, is one of the shallowest and most dangerous fallacies that has ever gained credence among men.

Kentucky, occupying a central position in the Union, is now protected from the scourge of a foreign war, however much its ravages may waste the towns and cities upon our coasts, or the commerce upon our seas; but as a member of the Southern Confederacy, she would be a frontier state, and necessarily the victim of those border feuds and conflicts which have become proverbial in history alike for their fierceness and frequency. The people of the South now sleep quietly in their beds, while there is not a home in infatuated and miguided Virginia that is not filled with the alarms and oppressed by the terrors of war. In the fate of the ancient commonwealth, dragged to the altar of sacrifice by those who should have stood between her bosom and every foe, Kentucky may read her own. *No wonder, therefore, that she has been so coaxingly besought to unite her fortunes with those of the South, and to lay down the bodies of her chivalric sons as a breastwork, behind which the Southern people may be sheltered.* Even as attached to the Southern Confederacy, she would be weak for all the purposes of self-protection, as compared with her present position. But amid the mutations incident to such a helpless and disintegrating league, Kentucky would probably soon find herself adhering to a mere fiagment of the Confederacy, or it may be standing entirely alone, in the presence of tiers of free states, with populations exceeding, by many millions, her own. Feeble states, thus separated from powerful and warlike neighbors by ideal boundaries, or by fears as easily traversed as rivulets, are as insects that feed upon the lion's lip—liable at every moment to be crushed. The recorded doom of multitudes of such, has left us a warning too solemn and impressive to be disregarded.

Kentucky now scarcely feels the contribution she makes to support the government of the United States, but as a member of the Southern Confederacy, of whose policy free trade will be a cardinal principle, she will be burdened with direct taxation to the amount of double, or, it may be, triple or quadruple that which she now pays into her own treasury. Superadded to this will be required from her her share of those vast outlays necessary for the creation of a navy, the erection of forts and custom-houses along a frontier of several thousand miles; and for the maintenance of that large standing army which will be indispensable at once for her safety, and for imparting to the new government that strong military character which, it has been openly avowed, the peculiar institutions of the South will inexorably demand.

Kentucky now enjoys for her peculiar institution the protection of the Fugitive Slave law, loyally enforced by the government, and it is this law, effective in its power of recapture, but infinitely more potent in its moral agency in preventing the escape of slaves, that alone saves that institution in the border states from utter extinction. She cannot carry this law with her into the new Confederacy. She will, virtually, have Canada brought to her doors in the form of free states, whose population, relieved of all moral and constitutional obligations to deliver up fugitive slaves, will stand with open arms, inviting and welcoming them, and defending them, if need be, at the point of the bayonet. Under such influences, slavery will perish rapidly pass away in Kentucky, as a ball of snow would melt in a summer's sun.

Kentucky, in her soul, abhors the African slave-trade, and turns away with unspeakable horror and loathing from the red altars of King Dahomey. *But although this traffic has been temporarily interdicted by the seceded states, it is well understood that this step has been taken as a mere measure of policy for the purpose of impressing the border states, and of conciliating the European powers. The ultimate legalization of this trade, by a republic professing to be based upon African servitude, must follow as certainly as does the conclusion from the premises of a mathematical proposition.* Is Kentucky prepared to see the hand upon the dial-plate of her civilization rudely thrust back a century, and to stand before the world the confessed champion of the African slave-hunter? Is she, with her unsullied fame, ready to become a pander to the rapacity of the African slave-trader, who burdens the very winds of the sea with the moans of the wretched captives whose limbs he has loaded with chains, and whose hearts he has broken? I do not, I cannot, believe it.

For this catalogue of what Kentucky must suffer in abandoning her present honored and secure position, and becoming a member of the Southern Confederacy, what will be her indemnity? Nothing, absolutely nothing. The ill-woven ambition of some of her sons may possibly reach the Presidency of the new republic; that is all. Alas! alas! for that dream of the Presidency of a Southern republic, which has disturbed so many pillows in the South, and perhaps some in the West, also, and whose lurid light, like a demon's torch, is leading a nation to perdition!

The clamor that in insisting upon the South obeying the laws, the great principle that all popular governments rest upon the consent of the governed is violated, should not receive a moment's consideration. Popular government does, indeed, rest upon the consent of the governed, but it is upon the consent, *not of all, but of a majority of the governed.* Criminals are every day punished, and made to obey the laws, certainly against their will, and no man supposes that the principle referred to is thereby invaded. A bill passed by the legislature, by the majority of a single vote only, though the constituents of all who voted against it should be, in fact as they are held to be in theory, opposed to its provisions, still is not the less operative as a law, and no right of self-government is thereby trampled upon. The clamor alluded to assumes that the states are separate and independent governments, and that laws enacted under the authority of all may be resisted and repealed at the pleasure of each. The people of the United States, so far as the powers of the general government are concerned, are a unit, and laws passed by a majority of all are binding upon all. The laws and constitution, however, which the South now resists, have been adopted by her sanction, and the right she now claims is that of a feeble minority to repeal what a majority has adopted. Nothing could be more fallacious.

Civil war, under all circumstances, is a terrible calamity, and yet, from the selfish ambition and wickedness of men, the best governments have not been able to escape it. In regarding that which has been forced upon the government of the United States, Kentucky should not look so much at the means which may be necessarily employed in its prosecution, as at the machinations by which this national tragedy has been brought upon us. When I look upon this bright land, a few months since so prosperous, so tranquil, and so free, and now behold it desolated by war, and the firesides of its thirty millions of people darkened, and their bosoms wrung with anguish, and know, as I do, that all this is the work of a score or two of men, who, over all this national ruin and despair, are preparing to carve with the sword their way to seats of permanent power, I cannot but feel that they are accumulating upon their soil an amount of guilt hardly equalled in all the atrocities of treason and homicide that have degraded the annals of our race from the foundations of the world. *Kentucky may rest well assured that this conflict, which is one of self-defence, will be pursued on the part of the Government in the paternal spirit in which a father seeks to reclaim his erring offspring. No conquest, no effusion of blood is sought. In sorrow, not in anger, the prayer of all is, that the end may be reached without loss of life or waste of property.* Among the most powerful instrumentalities relied on for re-establishing the authority of the government, is that of the Union sentiment of the South, sustained by a liberated press. It is now trodden to the earth under a reign of terrorism which has no parallel but in the worst days of the French revolution. The presence of the government will enable it to rebound and look its oppressors in the face. At present we are assured that in the seceded states no man expresses an opinion opposed to the revolution but at the hazard of his life and property. The only light which is admitted into political discussion is that which flashes from the sword or gleams from glistening bayonets. A few days since, one of the United State Senators from Virginia published a manifesto, in which he announces, with oracular solemnity and severity, that all citizens who would not vote for secession, but were in favor of the Union—not should or ought to—but "MUST leave the state." These words have in them decidedly the crack of the overseer's whip. The Senator evidently treats Virginia as a great negro quarter, in which the lash is the appropriate emblem of authority, and the only argument he will condescend to use. However the freemen of other parts of the state may abase themselves under the exercise of this insolent and proscriptive tyranny, should the Senator, with his scourge of slaves, endeavor to drive the people of Western Virginia from their homes, I will only say, in the language of the narrative of Gilpin's ride,

"May I be there to see!"

It would certainly prove a deeply interesting spectacle.

It is true that before this deliverance of the popular mind of the South from the threatenings and alarm which have subdued it can be accomplished, the remorseless agitators who have made this revolution, and now hold its reins, must be discarded alike from the public confidence and the public service. The country in its agony is feeling their power, and we well understand how difficult will be the task of overthrowing the ascendency they have secured. But the Union men of the South—believed to be in the majority in every seceded state, except, perhaps, South Carolina—aided by the presence of the government, will be fully equal to the emergency. Let these agitators perish, politically, if need be, by scores,

"A breath can unmake them as a breath has made;"

but destroy this republic, and

"Where is that Promethean heat
That can its light relume?"

Once entombed, when will the angel of the resurrection descend to the portals of its sepulchre? There is not a voice which comes to us from the cemetery of nations that does not answer: "Never, never!" Amid the torments of perturbed existence, we may have glimpses of rest and of freedom, as the maniac has glimpses of reason between the paroxysms of his madness, but we shall attain to neither national dignity nor national repose. We shall be a mass of jarring, warring, fragmentary states, enfeebled and demoralized, without power at home, or respectability abroad, and, like the republics of Mexico and South America, we will drift away on a shoreless and ensanguined sea of civil commotion, from which, if the teachings of history are to be trusted, we shall finally be rescued by the iron hand of some military wrecker, who will coin the shattered elements of our greatness and of our strength in a diadem and a throne. Said M. FOULD, the great French statesman, to an American citizen, a few weeks since: "Your republic is dead, and it is probably the last the world will ever see. You will have a reign of terrorism, and after that two or three monarchies." All this may be verified should this revolution succeed.

Let us, then, twine each thread of the glorious tissue of our country's flag about our heart-strings, and looking upon our homes and catching the spirit that breathes upon us from the battle-fields of our fathers, let us resolve, that, come weal or woe, we will, in life and in death, now and forever, stand by the stars and the stripes. They have floated over our cradles, let it be our prayer and our struggle that they shall float over our graves. They have been unfurled from the snows of Canada to the plains of New Orleans, to the halls of the Montezumas, and amid the solitudes of every sea; and everywhere, as the luminous symbol of resistless and beneficent power, they have led the brave and the free to victory and to glory. It has been my fortune to look upon this flag in foreign lands, and amid the gloom of an oriental despotism, and right well do I know, by contrast, how bright are its stars, and how sublime are its inspirations! If this banner, the emblem for us of all that is grand in human history, and of all that is transporting in human hope, is to be sacrificed on the altars of a Satanic ambition, and thus disappear forever amid the night and tempest of revolution, then will I feel—and who shall estimate the desolation of that feeling?—that the sun has indeed been stricken from the sky of our lives, and that henceforth we shall be but wanderers and outcasts, with naught but the bread of sorrow and penury for our lips, and with hands ever outstretched in feebleness and supplication, on which, in any hour, a military tyrant may rivet the fetters of a despairing bondage. May God in his infinite mercy save you and me, and the land we so much love, from the doom of such a degradation.

No contest so momentous as this has arisen in human history, for, amid all the conflicts of men and of nations, the life of no such government as ours has ever been at stake. Our fathers won our independence by the blood and the sacrifices of a seven years' war, and we have maintained it against the assaults of the greatest power upon the earth; and the question now is, whether we are to perish by our own hands, and have the epitaph of suicide written upon our tomb? The ordeal through which we are passing must involve immense suffering and losses for us all, but the expenditure of not merely hundreds of millions, but of billions of treasure, will be well made, if the result will be the preservation of our institutions.

Could my voice reach every dwelling in Kentucky, I would implore its inmates—if they would not have the rivers of their prosperity shrink away, as do unfed streams beneath the summer heats—to rouse themselves from their lethargy, and fly to the rescue of their country, before it is everlastingly too late. Man should appeal to man, and neighborhood to neighborhood, until the electric fires of patriotism shall flash from heart to heart in one unbroken current throughout the land. It is a time in which the workshop, the office, the counting-house, and the field, may well be abandoned for the solemn duty that is upon us, for all these toils will but bring treasure, not for ourselves, but for the spoiler, if this revolution is not arrested.

We are all, with our every earthly interest, embarked in mid-ocean on the same common deck. The howl of the storm is in our ears, and "the lightning's red glare is painting hell on the sky;" while the noble ship pitches and rolls under the lashings of the waves, the cry is heard that she has sprung a leak at many points, and that the rushing waters are mounting rapidly in the hold. The man who, in such an hour, will not work at the pumps, is either a maniac or a monster.

Sincerely yours,

JOSEPH HOLT.

www.ingramcontent.com/pod-product-compliance
Lightning Source LLC
LaVergne TN
LVHW011136110826
845150LV00008B/2378

* 9 7 8 1 4 1 8 1 9 3 9 5 9 *